Adventure Beneath the Sea

Living in an Underwater Science Station

Kenneth Mallory

Photographs by Brian Skerry

BOYDS MILLS PRESS
Honesdale, Pennsylvania

For Greg, Les, and James, who are leading the way. —*K.M.*

For Katherine and Caroline. May you always remain
curious and treasure the natural world. —*B.S.*

Text copyright © 2010 by Kenneth Mallory
Photographs copyright © 2010 by Brian Skerry

Boyds Mills Press, Inc.
815 Church Street
Honesdale, Pennsylvania 18431
Printed in the United States of America

ISBN: 978-1-59078-607-9

Library of Congress Control Number: 2010925565

First edition
The text of this book is set in 12-point Palatino.

10 9 8 7 6 5 4 3 2 1

Crowds of fishes cling to the safety of the Aquarius habitat.

CONTENTS

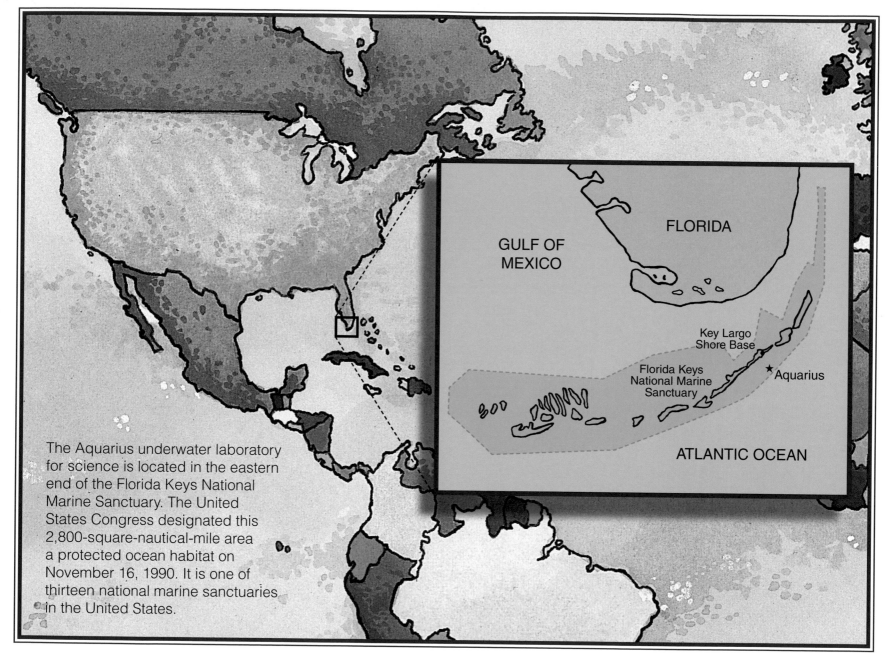

The Aquarius underwater laboratory for science is located in the eastern end of the Florida Keys National Marine Sanctuary. The United States Congress designated this 2,800-square-nautical-mile area a protected ocean habitat on November 16, 1990. It is one of thirteen national marine sanctuaries in the United States.

4

Introduction

Imagine what it would be like to live on a coral reef sixty feet deep in the Atlantic Ocean. Like a fish, you could spend your days dodging and darting among branches of coral and sponge. You'd see tiny shrimp, striped like candy canes, scurrying over the surface of the reef. Curious turtles and sparkling squid would glide through the water above. Below you, sea stars would crawl among the multicolored seaweeds and tiny worms that sprout feathery crowns.

Breathing would be easy, and the pressure of the water wouldn't bother you much at all. Sound too good to be true? Well, it is true, thanks to Aquarius—a scientific research station in the Florida Keys National Marine Sanctuary just off the southeastern coast of Florida.

Adventure Beneath the Sea tells the story of my seven-day mission living within a steel cylinder about the size of a large mobile home. Called Aquarius, my home away from home was just big enough to fit five other companions. Every day we used scuba equipment and special computer "tags" to follow fishes around the in coral reef home.

The goal of our project was to study where the animals of this reef—called Conch Reef—go night and day. Were the creatures that patrolled here just daily visitors who later traveled to other reefs? Or was Conch Reef a permanent home they depended on for survival?

If we could learn more about the reef creatures' daily habits, we might be able to protect them where they live. We might save them from being overfished. Living among them day and night using the Aquarius habitat would be a key to our mission's success.

Worldwide, coral reefs such as this one in Jamaica are home to an awe-inspiring array of living things. Twenty to 40 percent of all ocean species live in coral reefs.

Les Kaufman examines an elkhorn coral formation on a Jamaican reef.

An invertebrate called a Christmas tree worm displays its feathery plume, which captures food floating in the water.

Arrow crabs such as this one hide in the nooks and crannies of Aquarius.

Staghorn coral grows on a Jamaican coral reef.

A school of schoolmaster snappers. This group remained close to the habitat for the entire seven days of the fish-tagging mission.

Chapter 1

An Underwater Space Station

NOAA's Aquarius is the world's only active underwater research station. (NOAA is the National Oceanic and Atmospheric Administration.) If you want to know what it might be like living in space, you don't have to travel thousands of miles in a spaceship. Aquarius has many of the same conditions.

In an environment that doesn't allow for mistakes, a seemingly routine dive can turn into a life-threatening experience. Scuba divers experience weightlessness while swimming on the reef. Aquarius divers need to go through reentry before returning to normal life on the surface, much as astronauts do when returning from space. (See "Why Pressure Matters" on page 27.) And living in a small space requires everyone to get along. (Think of a small school classroom—but you can't go home.) In fact, NASA sends many of its astronauts to NOAA's Aquarius for "extreme environment" training.

Our home beneath the sea was a pressure-resistant steel cylinder. It's called Aquarius after the nighttime constellation that

Greg Stone gazes out of the bunk-room view port as he sips morning coffee.

means "water carrier." I like to think it's a mobile home someone has driven into the ocean, where it rests in place. Aquarius is 43 feet long and 9 feet in diameter.

With six aquanauts aboard, 9 feet was never wide enough. We had to "squeeze" past one another as we moved about inside.

Called a habitat because it is a self-contained space for living, Aquarius depends on a life-support platform that floats on the surface above. The Life Support Buoy, as it is called, is 30 feet in diameter. It is so large because it contains instruments and machines and communicates with Mission Control back on land. The buoy's compressors, as well as a set of large metal cylinders on the sea floor, produce a steady flow of air whose pressure is adjusted to keep seawater out.

During our mission, two cameras inside Aquarius and two cameras outside sent pictures back to support staff so they could keep track of us night and day. They even let us see the same images that were sent to computers everywhere on the Internet. Facebook, anyone?

A series of instruments monitors the temperature, oxygen, and carbon dioxide inside the habitat. A single large bundle of cable wires and hoses connects Aquarius and the Life Support Buoy like a huge umbilical cord.

The Life Support Buoy floats above the Aquarius habitat and provides communications and compressed air for the aquanauts 60 feet below.

Aquarius
The World's Only Underwater Laboratory for Science

Built in 1986, Aquarius began operation in St. Croix, U.S. Virgin Islands, in 1988. After thirteen successful missions there, Hurricane Hugo required the habitat be repaired and rebuilt. Since 1992, Aquarius has been located in the Florida Keys National Marine Sanctuary.

After twenty missions in Florida's Conch Reef, Aquarius was given a makeover. Today, missions run from April to November to avoid cold winter waters and for maintenance—usually eight missions a year. Aquarius is key to conducting science that helps us understand life on a coral reef. Besides tracking fish movement, which is the mission described in this book, Aquarius research teams monitor ocean acidification, the effects of global climate change, and the role sponges play in maintaining the reef.

Ready to Move In?

The Aquarius Undersea Laboratory . . .

- is an 80-ton cylindrical steel chamber made of three-quarter-inch-thick steel—43 feet long, 9 feet in diameter (If it wasn't attached to its 120-ton baseplate, it would float.)
- lies in 60 feet of water at the base of Conch Reef in the Florida Keys National Marine Sanctuary
- has eight exterior view ports

- houses six aquanauts at a time for one- to two-week missions
- is made up of two pressurized compartments, or "locks," with separate life-support controls and communications
- has backup high-pressure air, oxygen, CO_2 removal, and medical supplies

A side-view of the Aquarius habitat shows the emergency gazebo (white structure, far right) with a huge pocket of air inside, where divers can go to talk to one another. The habitat view port at the center looks in on the work/eating table within.

Chapter 2

Our Mission: Where Do the Fishes Go?

Greg Stone of the New England Aquarium was mission commander. He is a burly, bearded man with a ready laugh and a lifetime of experience exploring the ocean. Once we arrived at Mission Control in Key Largo, Florida, Greg divided our team into two groups.

The first team took a fishing boat to the reef where Aquarius is located, four miles offshore. This team spent the first days of the mission catching and tagging fishes using long lines cast from the boat.

When biologists Les Kaufman and James Lindholm caught the fishes they wanted to track later—in this case yellowtail snapper and black grouper—they made a small slit the width of a fingernail beneath each fish's belly. Didn't this hurt the fish? Not after it had been soaked in a bath of chemicals so it wouldn't feel the pain. Inside the fish, they placed a small computer tag and then closed the wound with some carefully sewn stitches. Sound

Top: James Lindholm holds an anesthetized black grouper following surgery to implant a pinger tag.

Bottom: Ken Mallory cleans his scuba mask inside Aquarius while Greg Stone (left) and aquanaut Craig Taylor discuss the morning dive.

Tim Gallagher, one of several trainers during preparation for living in the Aquarius habitat, does a final check on scuba tanks before the author and photographer visit the habitat for the first time.

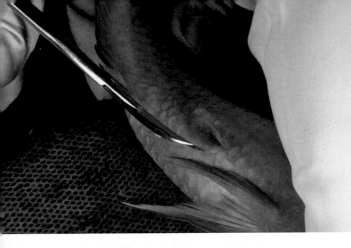

These blunt-end scissors were used to open the abdominal cavity after a scalpel had made the first cut.

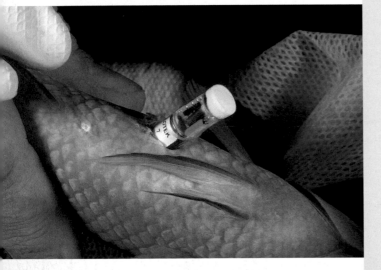

A Lotek pinger is about to be inserted into the cavity beneath this fish's stomach. Once inside the fish, the tag sends information to listening stations placed around Conch Reef.

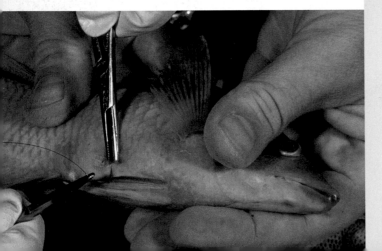

The fish looks like this after sutures have sewn the wound closed.

pulses produced by the tag—also called a pinger—would help divers follow the fish around the reef. Later, working underwater, Les and Greg used another kind of sound-making tag that beeped faster.

Once the surgery was over, a team of two divers took the fish with them as they swam down to the sea floor, then released it. Scientists onshore and later in Aquarius could track the fish. A series of listening stations placed around Conch Reef detected pulses from the tag, revealing the fish's movements. That will eventually help conservation biologists design marine protected areas to shelter heavily hunted fishes.

I was part of the second team of divers, called aquanauts. We stayed in Aquarius for the weeklong mission. Besides Greg and me, the team included *National Geographic* photographer Brian Skerry and a trustee of the Wildlife Conservation Society, Craig Taylor. Aquarius technician Jim Buckley and U.S. Navy Dive Doctor Christian Peterson rounded out the habitat team. In case of an accident, it was comforting to know that a physician skilled in emergency medicine was also on board.

Our team were humans living like fishes. Once we reached the underwater laboratory, the only limit to the time we spent exploring the reef was the amount of air stored in our scuba tanks. (*Scuba* stands for "self-contained underwater breathing apparatus.")

After surgically implanting a computer tag, James Lindholm swims his patient around to make sure it gets enough oxygen and to help it begin to swim on its own.

Chapter 3

The Adventure Begins . . . with Training

We aren't ready to dive to Aquarius yet. First, we have a lot to learn.

Our two trainers, Tim Gallagher and Mark "Otter" Hulsbeck, introduce themselves this morning. Tim is a dive specialist from Fort Collins, Colorado. He looks as if he just came back from running a triathlon. Otter is a gentle native Floridian with a full reddish-blond beard, long blond hair, and a tiny, sparkling-stone earring. He spent his time in the Navy on a rescue helicopter. Tim and Otter will be our teachers as we get to know Aquarius and the survival skills we will need to live underwater.

We spend some of our first four days testing our swimming and diving skills. Our training begins in a nearby hotel pool. Can we swim the length of a swimming pool underwater? Can we swim ten laps (400 yards) without fins and goggles? Can we stay afloat with our arms raised out of the water for fifteen minutes?

Aquarius trainer Tim Gallagher leads an aquanaut from an earlier mission in a session on how to use expedition lines arrayed around the habitat.

Tim Gallagher and Otter Hulsbeck run a training session for a different mission on the Aquarius habitat.

Can we give artificial respiration to a buddy floating in the water? If we pass this test, we can move on to the rest of the training.

Otter reminds us that once we have settled in our Aquarius home, we can't go back to the surface until after a long decompression. If we get lost underwater, rising to the surface would be dangerous and possibly deadly. For the next few days, we will learn what to do if we get lost.

On the third day, we aquanauts and our trainers take a dive boat to a part of Conch Reef close to Aquarius. For me, this is the first scary test. Under thirty feet of water, Otter tells me to take off my swimming mask. Ouch! My blurry eyes feel a stinging sensation that gets worse with every blink. Without the mask, I start to breathe through my nose instead of my mouthpiece—not a good idea underwater! I have to pinch my nose to stop myself from swallowing the ocean.

The visibility is so poor that I can barely see the hands in front of my face. Otter pushes an underwater chalkboard in front of my blurry eyes. Big letters made with a grease pen say:

NOW FIND YOUR WAY
BACK TO THE HABITAT

Gulp!

To prepare for poor vision in a sudden storm, we learn to rely on a network of safety ropes. Like threads of a spider's web, they branch out thousands of feet to emergency way stations, similar to hikers' warming huts. The safety ropes in turn contain plastic arrowheads, one embedded every thirty feet or so. All arrows point back to the habitat. As long as we can feel the direction the arrowheads are pointing, we can find our way back to Aquarius.

After a few false starts, I locate the first arrow on the safety line nearby. I'm sure Otter is still watching. So I desperately point in the direction of Aquarius, as if to say, "Please! Please! I know the way home! Can I please have my mask back now?"

I can't see Otter's expression. But I'm sure I'm not the first aquanaut who's finished this test with his eyes still stinging—and a healthy respect for what it takes to stay safe on an Aquarius mission.

One of the diving bells, also called way stations, that sit near the Aquarius habitat offers aquanauts the opportunity to take off their scuba masks and talk to one another. Air pressure inside keeps the water out. The diving bells are also safe havens in case of emergencies.

Habitat History
Starfish House, Sealab, and Others

The dream that humans could explore, work, and live underwater has existed since the beginning of recorded history. Leonardo da Vinci designed a breathing tube and an underwater mask in the 1500s. In the 1930s, explorer and naturalist William Beebe and inventor Otis Barton made a series of dives squeezed into a cast-steel cylinder less than five feet in diameter. Their deepest dive was more than three thousand feet. Designers and dreamers forecast vast cities under the ocean where citizens would farm food from the sea and escape from crowded cities on land.

Undersea explorer Jacques Cousteau was one of the first to build underwater structures called habitats. In 1943, Cousteau and Émile Gagnan worked together to invent the Aqualung, which was the forerunner for today's scuba tank. In 1962, as part of a program called Conshelf I, two "oceanauts" spent a week off the coast of Marseille, France, in a steel cylinder in thirty feet of water.

Conshelf II followed soon after, in the Red Sea. Cousteau called it an explorers' village. Its main living quarters, Starfish House, looked like a fat starfish wrapped in a steel skin. Aquanauts zoomed about the surrounding coral reef in a two-person submarine shaped like a flying saucer. Conshelf II also deployed a cylindrical chamber for two called Deep Cabin, traveling to depths of ninety feet and more.

While Cousteau was hard at work in France, an American Navy captain, Dr. George Bond ("Papa Topside") was completing his own experiments on how the human body copes with the effects of diving underwater for extended periods of time. His work on "saturation diving"—how breathing gases are absorbed in the human body under pressure—led to inventor Edwin Link's Man-in-the-Sea experiments and to Sealab I, the Navy's first underwater habitat, built in 1964.

This early work by Cousteau and Papa Topside, among other scientists, opened a new world of possibilities for living and working under the sea. Their work paved the way for a flurry of habitat designs built around the world that flourished in the early 1960s. More than sixty-five habitat programs have come and gone since the beginning of that decade. Together with Hydrolab (discontinued), NOAA's Aquarius is one of the most successful underwater laboratory programs in the history of underwater living.

Hydrolab, an American-designed structure built by Perry Submarine in 1966 and shown here off Grand Bahama Island. By 1968, three scientists had spent fifty hours inside at a depth of fifty feet.

1962
Man-in-Sea I
Conshelf I

1963
Conshelf II Deep Cabin
Conshelf II Starfish House

1964
SPID (Submersible Portable
    Inflatable Dwelling)
Sealab I

1965
Sealab II
Conshelf III

1966
Hydrolab
Caribe I
Bentos 300

1968
Edalhab
Chernomor I
Hebros II

1969
Tektite
Sealab III
Helgoland I
Chernomor II
Atlantik
Aegir

1971
Helgoland II
La Chalupa
Asteria

1986
Aquarius

Chapter 4

Life Inside Aquarius

This morning, Tim takes us out in the thirty-foot-long fast-response patrol boat *Manta* for our first visit to Aquarius. The habitat lies four miles off the Florida Keys coast, nine miles and a fifteen-minute boat ride from headquarters. By now, we are familiar with our twin scuba tanks; they carry twice as much air as most diving tanks do.

The day is sunny with a light breeze. After donning our wet suits and scuba tanks, we enter the water and do last-minute safety checks while bobbing at the surface. Waiting in the ocean swells is always the hardest part for me. All that ocean rock and roll makes my stomach queasy. Just in time, Tim gives a signal sending Brian, Craig, Greg, and me on our descent to the coral reef sixty feet below.

We dive, following the thick cable that stretches from the Life Support Buoy to the habitat. Sponges encrust the outside of Aquarius in a patchwork of reds, yellows, and greens. Long pipes, cylinders, and cables carrying electricity, water, and cold air for

Top: Schools of fish gather around the Aquarius habitat.
Middle: A small fish called a blenny uses the structure that supports Aquarius to find protection and to hunt for food.
Bottom: A fish called a sergeant major guards its nest of eggs placed along the wall of the Aquarius habitat.

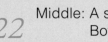

air conditioning flank the sides of the habitat. Schools of brightly colored fishes flow in and out of spaces in the 118-ton support cradle that secures the habitat to the reef floor.

As we approach one end of our future home beneath the sea, we peer like fish into the bunk-room view port. How will I ever fall asleep in such tightly packed quarters? Narrow bunks provide just enough space for six aquanauts, three beds to a side. An Aquarius technician inside greets us with a wave and a smile. But this is as close as our trainers will let us get for now.

First Entry

This morning, after three more days of training, we enter Aquarius for the first time. We don't stay very long, only about forty-five minutes. But it gives us a chance to see how it would feel to live like sardines in a can.

Based on the good-natured ribbing my bunkmates had given me the night before—they said I was screaming in my sleep!—I knew I must have been more than a little nervous. I try to remember how relaxed I felt during a deep-sea submarine dive a few months earlier. What that experience didn't tell me, however, was how I'd respond to a week in confined quarters with no dry land in sight.

It takes about five minutes for all of us to swim down to the entrance of the habitat. As I pop my head up into

A diver brings a pressurized pot containing clothes and sensitive scientific instruments into the Aquarius moon pool.

the air of the entryway, called the moon pool, I feel as if
I have entered a mudroom after a heavy rain. The air is
damp, and the surrounding pressure makes my head feel
congested. A plastic grating gives us a platform to stow
our diving gear.

     While we undo the harnesses that secure the tanks
of air on our backs, Tim warns us about tiny octopuses.
"They love to curl up and hide inside scuba regulators
[mouthpieces] left hanging in the water in the
moon-pool storage area," he says. "If you don't shake
them loose, they'll give you a nasty bite."

     Inside the habitat for the first time, Greg Stone
and I celebrate our arrival with slightly high-pitched
Donald Duck voices—the result of higher-than-normal
air pressure on our vocal cords. "Did you see that
barracuda?" quacks Greg. We kneel on a platform inside
the moon pool. Our every word sends an echo
bouncing around the steel walls. We have to speak slowly
and repeat ourselves often.

     A steel-rung ladder leads to a larger room, the wet
porch, with a sink and a shower. Most of the room,
however, is taken up with the valves and instruments for

Divers enter and exit Aquarius through the moon pool.
Air pressure from the habitat keeps water out of the aquanauts' living quarters.

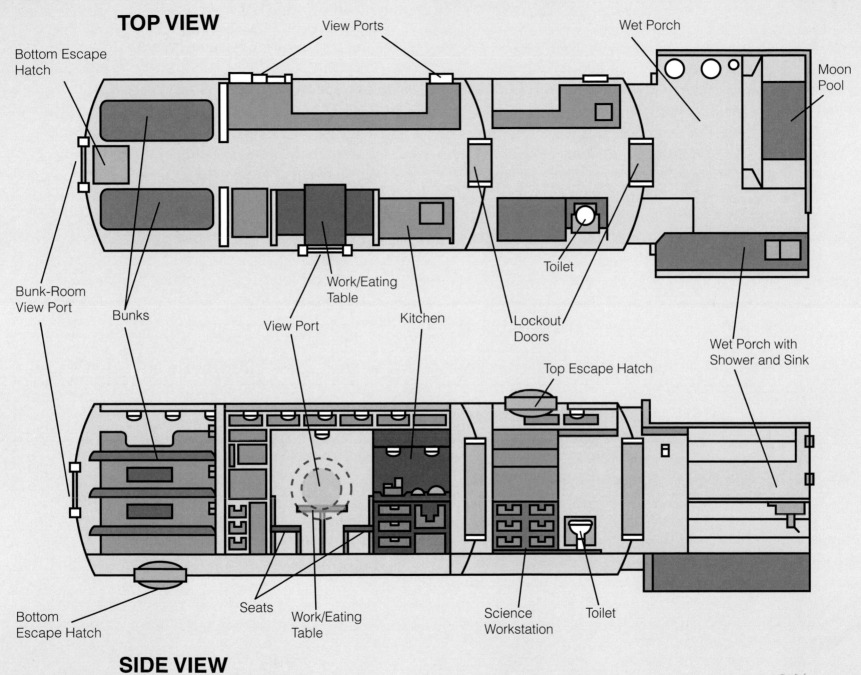

TOP VIEW

View Ports

Wet Porch

Bottom Escape Hatch

Moon Pool

Bunk-Room View Port

Bunks

Work/Eating Table

View Port

Kitchen

Lockout Doors

Toilet

Wet Porch with Shower and Sink

Top Escape Hatch

Bottom Escape Hatch

Seats

Work/Eating Table

Science Workstation

Toilet

SIDE VIEW

25

air supply to the habitat and air we can add to our scuba tanks. Like cars pulling into a gas station, we will be able to pass a cable up to one of the Aquarius technicians. Five minutes later, we can swim off again with our tanks refilled with air.

Greg and I laugh as we notice schools of fish gathered in the small view ports. We are the ones being watched, as if we are inside an aquarium rather than the other way around.

Once we have showered, to get rid of the salt water, and dried off, Otter leads us to a lockout door, like those found in submarines. Instead of turning a wheel to open the door, he pushes a lever. With a brief, loud hiss, the door slides magically to one side. Now we can see the banks of computers and controls that are the heart of our new home. Beyond are a toilet, an equipment-storage and workroom, a sink, a microwave oven, dining table, a trash compactor, and six bunk beds, three to a side. I quickly choose one of the top bunks. I'd heard it is the best place to hear the noisy nightlife of snapping shrimp just on the other side of the bedroom ceiling.

Inside Aquarius

Otter leads us into the first of two pressurized compartments called locks. It lies just beyond the wet porch. A second lock includes the rest of Aquarius that contains the kitchen and bunk room. The compartments are called locks because each room can be sealed off from the other if a fire, a leak, or other hazard occurs.

Although there are eight view ports in all, the biggest and most inviting is opposite the shiny steel table at the center of the Aquarius habitat—it's just like the submarine windows I remember from Jules Verne's book *Twenty Thousand Leagues Under the Sea*.

The Aquarius technicians will monitor all of the vital signs of habitat life: temperature, humidity, air pressure, and carbon dioxide. But Otter wants us to know what all the valves and instruments do in case something happens to the crew.

Every breath we exhale puts the waste gas carbon dioxide (CO_2) into the air around us. Too much CO_2 can lead to carbon-dioxide poisoning, making it difficult to breathe, even life threatening. Air filters called carbon-dioxide scrubbers sit in containers along one of the instrument panels to absorb excess gas.

We learn where to find oxygen masks and bottles and an escape hatch in the floor of the bunk room, which we can open to escape in emergencies. "If a fire breaks out in another part of the habitat," Otter explains, "there's an emergency rope hanging right under the trapdoor. Just use the rope to swim to the gazebo." The gazebo is a roofed shelter at the side of the wet porch where we entered the habitat. The oxygen bottles would give us plenty of air for the escape. And once we get inside it, the gazebo stores lots more air to breathe in emergencies.

Next we see the microwave oven, the hot-water dispenser, and the bins where our food is stored in sealed foil

Why Pressure Matters

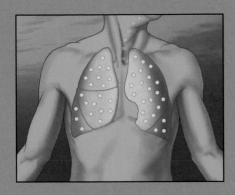

Breathing at Sea Level
At normal air pressure (14.7 pounds per square inch), nitrogen gas moves harmlessly in and out of the lungs along with the oxygen needed to sustain life.

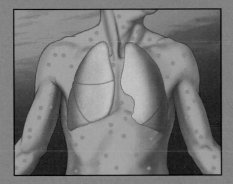

Breathing While Diving
During a deep dive, the pressure may be two or three times normal or more. High pressure forces nitrogen gas to dissolve into a diver's blood and other tissues.

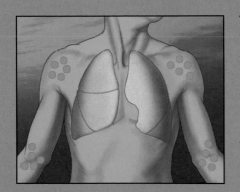

The Bends
Rising too fast reduces the pressure quickly. Nitrogen bubbles form in the blood and become stuck in the joints and elsewhere, causing intense pain and sometimes death.

Although we hardly notice, air has weight and produces pressure—14.7 pounds per square inch at sea level. This constant push is called atmospheric pressure. Underwater, the weight from air and water is much greater. At the entrance to the Aquarius habitat—47 feet below—the pressure is about two and one-half times surface pressure.

The pressure squeezes your lungs like a tight T-shirt, making breathing difficult. It presses in on your eardrums and your sinuses. Most important, it forces nitrogen and other gases from the air into the tissues of your body, especially your blood.

Trouble comes when divers return to the surface after a long dive. If they swim up too quickly, tiny nitrogen bubbles form inside their bodies.

Divers call this life-threatening condition the bends because nitrogen bubbles sometimes get caught in joints (where our bodies bend), inflicting pain. The bubbles can also block blood flow and even cause a heart attack.

One way to avoid the bends is to surface very slowly. This approach lets gases seep out naturally. Decompression time can be as little as five to ten minutes after a dive. Or it can require hours, as it did for us after a week in Aquarius. After twenty-four hours in the habitat, it doesn't matter how much longer you stay; the decompression time of 16.5 hours stays the same.

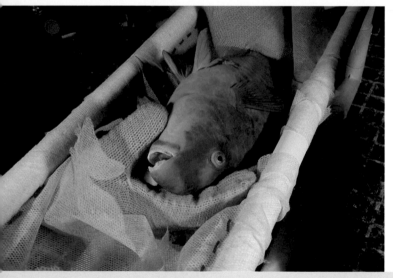

bags. Just add hot water to the freeze-dried food: breakfast, lunch, and dinner.

But for technology junkies like me, the best is yet to come. Wireless communication links ship to shore for Internet access, video conferencing, telephone calls, and even voice to and from divers in the water. We are supplied with the latest and best in communication wizardry.

The last room we see contains the bunks that will pack us tightly at the far end of Aquarius. Separated by a curtain from the rest of the habitat, foam-pad mattresses are stacked in shelves, one above the other. Since I have already been caught yelling in my sleep earlier during training, I worry my bunkmates will be listening closely.

Almost Live on the Internet

Over the years, Aquarius has made it possible for Internet users to see the same images as Mission Control. Every mission today allows aquanauts' friends and loved ones a chance to glimpse what it is like living with the fishes. Since we know friends and family are watching, we sometimes jockey for the best place to be seen at the dining-room table.

Although Internet users can't hear habitat voices, aquanauts

Top: Greg Stone attends to some of the fish caught in a trap near Aquarius. Once he decides which fish are good candidates for tagging, he takes them to Les Kaufman for the surgical implant.

Bottom: On a platform outside the moon pool, Les has rigged a makeshift operating table where he will operate on this fish, which has been put to sleep temporarily with underwater anesthetics.

make up for the silence by placing billboard signs on the cooler near the habitat's main camera. Messages that sometimes change daily let baseball fans celebrate ("Go, Red Sox!" and "Manny's number 1!") or offer personal greetings such as "Hi, Mom" and "Send food."

Computer Tags

Les Kaufman—the biologist who began our mission catching fishes from a boat—remains on land while the rest of us live in Aquarius. Since he is the most skilled fish surgeon, however, he comes aboard Aquarius each day, making dives to insert more computer tags into fishes.

With netting spread between a platform of plastic pipes, Les and Greg Stone fashion a makeshift operating table on the habitat porch. A few squirts of anesthesia into the fish's mouth puts the patient to sleep. Then Les inserts the second kind of pinger, called a Lotek tag. This gives the aquanaut trackers like Craig and me two kinds of signals to look for as we search the reef for fishes.

Greg and Les have to be on their best behavior since *National Geographic* photographer Brian Skerry is filming their every move. Les spent one and a half hours and tagged additional species of fishes. Among his favorite patients is a navy blue parrot fish.

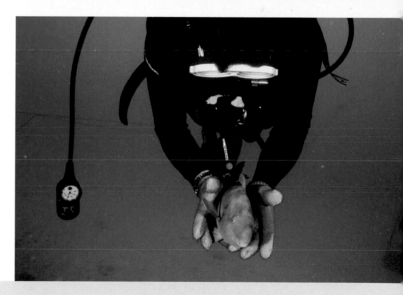

Top: A Lotek pinger is about to be inserted into the cavity beneath this fish's stomach. Once inside the fish, the tag sends information to listening stations placed around Conch Reef.

Bottom: After the operation, Les swims his patient around until it begins to swim on its own.

View-Port Visitors

When we aren't tagging fishes, we are busy watching them. Wednesday brings a new cast of characters to the dining-room view port. Creole wrasses arrive in squadrons, pacing back and forth in front of the window, often at high speed. With forked tails and tapered dark-blue bodies, Creole wrasses swim in tight-knit schools that seem to block out the sun.

On Thursday bluehead wrasses and schoolmasters replace Creole wrasses as the most frequent visitors. But by Friday, it seems as if the biggest aggressors of the reef have shown up to examine us. A trio of six-foot-long tarpons—silvery, shiny game fish popular with the fishermen—parade in front of the view port with schooling precision. They don't just make a few casual passes; they look at me with threatening stares. They seem to say, "Go back to where you came from!"

Barracuda Patrols

Barracuda give me the creeps. I know they don't hunt humans to eat. But their toothy grins and their silent stalking still unnerve me. They lurk everywhere around the Aquarius laboratory. You can find them in the water column above you, peering down in twos and threes. In far greater numbers—sometimes twenty or thirty—they laze motionless just above the sandy ocean floor. They prefer to hunt at dusk and dawn, but during the day they guard their territory.

Top: Photographer Brian Skerry watches fish through the view port.

Bottom: A barracuda patrols the Aquarius habitat, waiting for dusk, when it prefers to hunt.

Sergeant Majors

I love to watch the reef's tiny territorial defenders. Ten feet to the side of our dining-room view port lives a four-inch-long fish called a sergeant major. With black and white stripes that make him look as if he's escaped from a prison, he guards a patch of territory on one of the habitat's supporting girders. I think he's hoping to attract a mate, or maybe he's protecting some precious eggs.

Any fish or person who approaches his neighborhood—no matter how big or small—triggers a fierce display. Over and over he rushes toward the intruder, even taking nips to try to scare it away.

A line attached to Aquarius and reaching to a buoy at the surface sits close to the sergeant major's home. On days when the weather topside is making waves, the buoy line bobs up and down, and it sends the little fish into a frenzy. Since the bobbing and weaving of the buoy continue as long as the weather stays bad, there's little rest for the feisty and determined sergeant major.

Nature's Calling

During training, I'd heard some scary stories about the habitat's toilet. On the first day, I find out they are all true. Over the years, there have been many toilet jams and overflows. One time, before my stay, the toilet exploded from too much pressure. These days, we just do our business out in the ocean. It's natural for all the other animals in the ocean, so why not for us?

One by one, dressed only in our swimming trunks, each of us takes a turn swimming from the moon pool entrance to the gazebo ten feet away, where we can surface in a pocket of air. The dome-shaped structure serves as a way station where we can gather in case of a fire or other emergency in the habitat.

Here we can find a little bathroom privacy. Eager fish scavengers make sure there's nothing left behind. But watch out—sometimes they get a little too eager.

The Talking Sea

Lying in bed at night lets me focus on the sounds we live with every day in our underwater home. From the top bunk, the ceiling above me is alive with the crackle of thousands of tiny snapping shrimp.

Each of these inch-long creatures, also called pistol shrimp, is equipped with a monster-sized claw. As the shrimp snaps its giant claw shut, it produces a small bubble that explodes with a loud pop; it uses it to stun prey, communicate to other shrimp, and defend its territory. Thousands of these bubbles produce the snaps and crackles I hear above me.

The ocean is a surprisingly noisy place. Eight hundred times denser than air, water carries sounds quickly and far. Through water, sound travels about the length of fifteen football fields a second. That's five times faster than through the air. Marine animals use this to their advantage by producing telltale burps, clicks, whistles, booms, and moans to talk to one another.

Some kinds of fishes talk by rubbing their fin spines together. Others grind their teeth. Still others use muscles to vibrate an internal organ called the swim bladder. The thrumming sound it produces can broadcast a warning or attract a mate. It's a talent that has led scientists to name some of the fish "drums" or "croakers."

What's to Eat?

Eating in an underwater habitat has limitations. Aquanauts have to eat food that can be transported and stored easily. Although Aquarius has a cooler onboard, it is small and doesn't always keep foods cold enough to avoid spoiling. Most of what we eat is canned or freeze-dried. The milk has been treated with ultra-high temperature, which kills all bacteria and bacterial spores so that the milk won't spoil without refrigeration.

When scientists first built underwater habitats in the 1960s, aquanauts did all they could to make their food more appetizing. In the habitat he designed called Starfish House, famed French explorer Jacques Cousteau had hot meals sent down from the surface in pressure-resistant containers. He even served wine.

In one Russian habitat, an aquanaut received an angel food cake that his wife had baked for his birthday. By the time it was brought to habitat depth, the increased pressure had collapsed it to the thickness of a pancake!

While many of the foods we eat in Aquarius are the same as those available in the early days of underwater exploration, they are packaged and cooked a lot differently. Frying food in a skillet is forbidden because it would raise the temperature and humidity inside our little home. Besides, we don't have a conventional oven or stove.

We use a microwave oven instead. Or we add hot water to packages of freeze-dried food. One of our least-favorite meals is a breakfast of scrambled eggs and bacon. It is so tasteless, the only way we can eat it is to smother it with hot sauce.

Greg and I put on happy faces, pretending the food is simply delicious. We enjoy the candy bars and other junk food on hand, but what we crave are grapes and other fresh fruits, which would spoil in Aquarius. We find ourselves praying for visitors bearing these gifts from the world above.

On the Menu

A scientist on a different mission chooses his morning meal.

Here's a list of the foods we ate during our stay in Aquarius.

Dried apricots, bananas, and apples
Freeze-dried vegetarian entrée
Freeze-dried beef stroganoff
Freeze-dried scrambled eggs
Freeze-dried chicken Parmesan
Freeze-dried long-grain and wild rice
Mushroom pilaf
Minestrone soup
Pudding
Miso-Cup Delicious Vegetable Soup
Canned beef ravioli
Dry cereal in small boxes
Peanut butter

Ramen noodle soup, pork flavor
Chips
Nuts
Crackers
Peanuts
Cheese-and-peanut-butter crackers
Candy bars
Fig bars
Raisins
Ultra-high-temperature-treated milk
        (doesn't need refrigeration)
Hot sauce

Chapter 5

All in a Day's Work

Craig Taylor and I get up around six thirty a.m. to begin tracking fishes. We carry a hand-held device that reminds me of a laser tag pistol or a heavy-duty underwater flashlight. As we get close to a fish that has a computer tag tucked under its skin, numbers from 0 to 100 appear on the gun's video screen. The higher the number, the closer we are to a fish that's been tagged. How cool is that? It's like hunting for buried treasure.

Craig and I try to find as many tagged fishes as possible in our two-hour dives. We are looking for two different kinds of signals: One is for the fishes tagged from the fishing boat by team one early in the mission. The other signal—a more rapidly repeating *beep-beep*—means they are the Lotek tags we had inserted while living in Aquarius. For whatever reason, the Lotek tags are easier to follow.

The listening stations placed around Conch Reef record a visit each time a tagged fish comes within their range. But they

Top: Greg Stone shines an underwater flashlight as aquanaut Craig Taylor operates the instrument that picks up pinger sounds in fish that have been tagged.

Bottom: One of the coral reef's many grouper species hovers below the Aquarius habitat. This fish is called a goliath grouper, a kind of grouper that scientists hope to tag in the future.

can't tell the scientists how well the fish recover following the surgery. If we can get close and spend time observing, it will help future missions improve tagging success.

We head toward the northeast way station one thousand feet away. We travel along one of the emergency navigation lines. After a brief encounter with a curious turtle, we pick up a Lotek signal. It is in the same area where we had released a grouper almost a week earlier.

The signal gets stronger. At the edge of a coral cliff sits a well-camouflaged grouper staring back at us. It doesn't seem the slightest bit afraid. On its lower lip, which projects in front of the upper, is a slight tear from where the fishing hook had been removed. We feel as if we have found a lost friend. Even better: after ten minutes watching it move about the reef, we can see it's behaving normally.

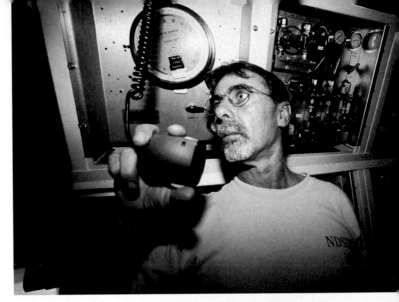

Lights Out

Greg and Craig are fifteen minutes into a night dive when the lights inside Aquarius suddenly go out. The familiar, soothing sound of the habitat's air-conditioner falls quiet.

"This doesn't look good," I mumble to myself, trying to calm my fears. We are sixty feet deep in the Atlantic Ocean. And returning to the surface isn't an option!

In the dim light of the emergency backup generator, Aquarius

Top: Aquarius technician Jim Buckley uses the ship-to-shore radio to tell Mission Control that the generator has stopped working and we are operating on emergency power.

Bottom: An unhappy crew of aquanauts—Greg Stone, Ken Mallory, and Craig Taylor—wait for the main power to come back on to replace emergency lighting after the generator shut down.

technician Jim Buckley picks up the ship-to-shore radio. He tries to contact Mission Control nine miles away.

Greg and Craig still have plenty of air left in their scuba tanks. But if they can't find Aquarius because its lights have gone out, they might have no choice but to surface.

After Jim gets off the phone with Mission Control, he sounds the siren Aquarius uses for emergencies. Yellow lights pulse on and off inside the habitat, shining on our worried faces. Inside the metal structure, the wailing of the siren throbs in our ears as it echoes off the steel walls.

If Greg and Craig can hear the siren, it will warn them to return to the habitat. As long as they can locate the spider web of expedition lines, they will be able to feel their way home.

Five minutes pass. Then ten. But it seems like much longer. Maybe Greg and Craig have less air than we think. Could something have gone wrong with their scuba tanks?

Just as I am beginning to think we might have to organize a search party, Greg and Craig appear at the moon pool entrance, exchanging glances of relief. The emergency isn't over, however. Jim Buckley thinks it might be a problem with the generator in the Life Support Buoy.

Greg Stone tries an unusual method of placing tags in fishes. Here, he searches for a moray eel that might take the bait.

He'll have to wait for a team of divers to confirm his suspicions. A long hour and lots of sweating later, the lights trip on. And much to our relief, the air-conditioner begins to stream cool air once again.

By now, we are all exhausted and ready for bed.

Going Fishing

One morning, I watch Greg Stone do something strange. As he hovers just over a patch of coral reef, he holds a fishing rod baited with a bologna sandwich in front of a moray eel. Inside the sandwich is a tiny $2,000 Lotek pinger. Instead of doing surgery to place the tag inside the eel, Greg has a better idea.

A moray eel doesn't like divers swimming too close. But because Greg dangled a lure from a safe distance ten feet above, the curious fish couldn't resist. With one giant chomp, the moray snaps the fishing line and swallows the bologna sandwich.

Back inside the Aquarius habitat, a computer has already picked up the *ping, ping, ping* sent out from the tag inside the eel's stomach. Moray eels hide in caves and crevices in the reef. This one apparently likes the hole where we found him. The computer signal confirms his whereabouts.

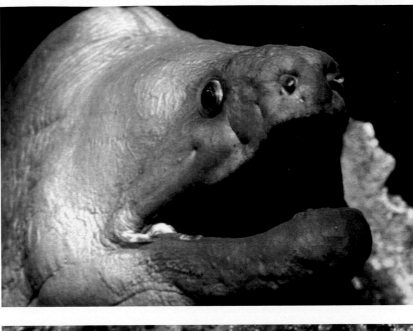

Moray eels like these find lots of food around the Aquarius habitat.

Chapter 6

The End of the Adventure

A week has passed since our first night in Aquarius. It is too early to know if the fishes we have been tracking remain in Conch Reef's marine protected area or if they travel far away.

But thanks to the series of listening stations that remain behind on the reef, we'll continue to track fishes even after we leave the habitat. For those of us who have taken part in the expedition, we decide it was a good beginning that will lead to similar missions in the future.

The final steps in the completion of our mission are to pack up and send our gear back to a boat waiting at the ocean surface. Big pressure-resistant pots a foot wide and nearly two feet deep keep clothing and scientific instruments dry and safe on the journey to the surface.

Then we go through nearly seventeen hours of decompression before we can leave.

We lie in our bunks and breathe from masks attached to small bottles of pure oxygen. Pure oxygen speeds up what's called

Aquarius technician Jim Buckley checks the contents of a pressurized pot about to be sent back to the surface.

off-gassing, the slow release of the nitrogen gas that has built up in our bloodstream after a week living sixty feet deep.

If we release the air pressure in the habitat too quickly, gas bubbles will clog the free flow of blood in our bodies, at joints, and to and from the heart. Otter tells me this has never happened to an aquanaut during all the years Aquarius has been in service. But we know we can never be careful enough.

Once the first hour of breathing pure oxygen is over, we are free to walk around the habitat. Some of us read books. Others play video games or go on the Internet to e-mail our friends. By the time seventeen hours have passed, the pressure inside Aquarius is the same as it is at the surface. An hour later, all six of us aquanauts have swum to the surface and are climbing onto a boat that will take us back to base.

Looking Back . . . and Forward

Our team of weary but happy aquanauts spent a final day reflecting on our underwater journey before we left for home. We knew we'd been privileged with an experience few others will ever have. But with this privilege and understanding comes responsibility. The world's oceans are in trouble. The wealth of fishes we

An Aquarius support diver ascends to the surface at the end of the mission with a pressure pot containing gear used in the weeklong stay underwater.

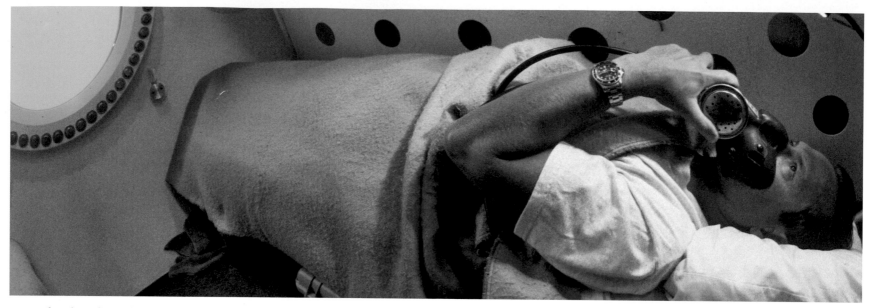

once had is fast disappearing. Our trip to Aquarius had taught us that marine sanctuaries might be one way to help us save the oceans as they should be.

The future of marine sanctuaries is filled with promise. The work that Les and James had done tagging fishes was but a small step in understanding how fishes live inside a coral reef. After six months of collecting information from the listening stations placed around Conch Reef, we found that yellowtail snappers and black groupers almost never left Conch Reef. If we could show that was true for other important fishes living here, we could make a good case for creating bigger and better sanctuaries.

The message hasn't been lost on Greg Stone. He's used the encouraging results of our Aquarius mission to help create the world's largest marine protected area in the Pacific Ocean—158,000 square nautical miles of ocean, or about fifty times the size of Yellowstone National Park. It's called the Phoenix Islands Protected Area and lies in the Pacific Ocean about 1,650 miles south-southwest of Hawaii.

And the same is true for Les and James. Both are now hard at work creating marine parks—from northern and southern California to Massachusetts and the Gulf of Maine.

And what about Brian and me? That's why we created this book.

During the first hour of the 16.5-hour decompression, aquanaut Craig Taylor breathes pure oxygen to get rid of nitrogen bubbles he has absorbed after being underwater for a week.

Coral Reefs in Danger

Tiny coral animals are the architects of the world's coral reefs. Each one is the size of the eraser at the end of a pencil, yet together they can create huge underwater cities. Each coral animal, or polyp, looks like a miniature sea anemone. Packed together, they form colonies called pillar, staghorn, leaf, or elkhorn coral, after shapes they resemble.

Coral reefs play a vital role in the health of the oceans. They provide living and hiding places for plants and animals that couldn't otherwise survive. They supply food for local fishermen. They protect shorelines from the crashing waves of coastal storms. They absorb and recycle carbon dioxide, a gas that contributes to global climate change.

Often called the rain forests of the sea, coral reefs contain between 20 and 40 percent of the 160,000 known marine species. Work by the Global Coral Reef Monitoring Network, however, shows that coral reefs are in decline. Overfishing and pollution from towns and cities are some of the reasons for the concern.

Even more alarming is the "bleaching" of corals due to global climate change or other causes. The coral animal lives in a sharing relationship with a single-celled plant—a type of alga that lives inside the coral and gives the coral its color. Through photosynthesis, the alga generates oxygen and nutrients that the coral uses. In turn, the coral provides the plant with carbon dioxide and

minerals. Thus, the coral and alga depend on each other for survival.

When coral animals are under stress—such as when the water temperature rises too high for too long—they eject their algal partners. Without the pigments in the algae, the coral reef looks pale or even white, which is the origin of the term *bleaching*. If the stress is not relieved and if the coral animals are not re-colonized by algae, the coral will die, the reef will deteriorate, and many sea creatures that depend on the reef will die.

We hope the work we did onboard Aquarius will help people appreciate a precious undersea world that is fast disappearing.

Close-up of coral animals, called coral polyps, that are responsible for creating the large limestone structures that make up a coral reef.

Acknowledgments

The author would like to thank the New England Aquarium, the National Oceanic and Atmospheric Administration (NOAA), and the University of North Carolina, Wilmington for making this book possible. Former vice president of Global Marine Programs at the New England Aquarium Greg Stone and former director of the Aquarius underwater laboratory Steven Miller were instrumental in seeing the need for this kind of book about scientists in the field, as was former New England Aquarium president, now president and CEO, Aquarium of the Pacific, Jerry Schubel. Thanks are due to current associate director of Aquarius, Otto Rutten; operations director Craig Cooper; and chief scientist Dr. Ellen Praeger for their helpful review of the manuscript; and to

science writer and editor Melissa Stewart for her editorial guidance. Brian Skerry contributed his immeasurably fine photography and good humor (thanks, Karen!) while my editor at Boyds Mills Press, Andy Boyles, and Amanda Lewis of the Doe Coover Agency pulled all the pieces into a coherent whole. Finally, the opportunity to explore the ocean with three good friends, Boston University professor Les Kaufman; the aforementioned Greg Stone, now Senior Vice President and Chief Scientist for Oceans, Conservation International; and photographer Brian Skerry will always be a treasure. With friends like these and marine sanctuary advocates Dr. James Lindholm and Dr. Sylvia Earle, the blue planet may ultimately thrive.

For More Information

BOOKS FOR YOUNG READERS

Earle, Sylvia A. *Dive! My Adventures in the Deep Frontier*. Washington, DC: National Geographic Society, 1999.

Earle, Sylvia A. *Coral Reefs*. Washington, DC: National Geographic Society, 2003.

Gaines, Richard. *The Explorers of the Undersea World*. New York: Chelsea House Publishers, 1994.

Lindop, Laurie. *Venturing the Deep Sea*. Minneapolis, MN: Twenty-First Century Books, 2006.

Lourie, Peter. *First Dive to Shark Dive*. Honesdale, PA: Boyds Mills Press, 2006.

Matsen, Brad. *The Incredible Record-Setting Deep-Sea Dive of the Bathysphere*. Berkeley Heights, NJ: Enslow Publishers, 2003.

Rhodes, Mary Jo. *Life on a Coral Reef*. New York: Children's Press, 2006.

Collard, Sneed B. III. *Lizard Island: Science and Scientists on Australia's Great Barrier Reef*. New York: Franklin Watts, 2000.

Collard, Sneed B. III. *One Night in the Coral Sea*. Watertown, MA: Charlesbridge Publishing, 2005.

Stewart, Melissa. *Extreme Coral Reef! Q&A*. New York: HarperCollins Publishers, 2008.

BOOKS FOR OLDER READERS

Miller, James W., and Ian G. Koblick. *Living and Working in the Sea*. 2nd ed. Flagstaff, AZ: Best Publishing Company, 1995.

Marx, Robert F. *The History of Underwater Exploration*. New York: Dover Publications, 1990.

WEB SITES*

Aquarius
uncw.edu/aquarius
Home page of the Aquarius undersea research station.

Magic Porthole
www.magicporthole.org
Web site devoted to coral reefs.

National Oceanic and Atmospheric Administration
www.noaa.gov
Web site of NOAA, which owns Aquarius.

Ocean World
oceanworld.tamu.edu/students/coral
Coral reef Web site at Texas A&M University.

2008 Coral Reef Educational Resources
coralreef.noaa.gov/education/educators/resourcecd

The National Undersea Research Center
www.uncw.edu/nurc

The Reef Check Foundation
www.reefcheck.org

Global Coral Reef Monitoring Network
www.gcrmn.org

Coral Reef News
www.sciencedaily.com/news/earth_climate/coral_reefs

Coral Reefs at Surfing the Net with Kids
www.surfnetkids.com/coralreef.htm

Coral Realm
library.thinkquest.org/25713

New England Aquarium Web site
www.neaq.org

*Active at time of publication

Glossary

Aqualung Name of a brand of **scuba** equipment.

aquanaut A person who has remained underwater at least twenty-four hours without coming to the surface. *Aqua* is Latin for water, and *naut* come from the Greek *nautes*, meaning sailor.

Aquarius The world's only underwater laboratory for science.

atmospheric pressure The force that the weight of Earth's atmosphere exerts. At sea level, this pressure is 14.7 pounds per square inch, on average.

bends (often *the bends*) A sometimes life-threatening condition that occurs in divers when they surface too soon after a long dive.

carbon dioxide (chemical formula CO_2) A chemical compound in Earth's atmosphere that is produced as a "waste gas" by many living things, including humans.

Conch Reef The coral reef where Aquarius is located, about nine miles south of Key Largo, in the Florida Keys.

Conshelf A series of underwater habitat experiments under the direction of French explorer Jacques Yves Cousteau, beginning in 1962.

coral bleaching A devastating rise in seawater temperature at a coral reef, which can kill the tiny animals that make coral formations.

coral polyp A tiny, soft-bodied animal that lives in sunny waters, filters minerals from seawater to build a hard skeleton around itself, and relies on a tiny alga plant inside it to give it energy through photosynthesis. Together, hundreds of thousands of coral polyps build the coral reef as they grow and multiply over many generations by anchoring their skeletons to rocks, to one another's skeletons, and to the skeletons of dead coral polyps.

coral reef An immense natural formation built up on the limestone skeletons of coral animals found only in the tropics. Coral reefs are home to between 20 and 40 percent of the 160,000 known marine species. Coral reefs are also among the earth's most threatened ecosystems.

croaker See **drumfish**.

decompression A gradual process of reducing the air pressure exerted on a diver, allowing any nitrogen dissolved in the bloodstream and body tissues to seep harmlessly out of those tissues before the diver reaches the surface.

drumfish (also *croaker*) A member of a family of fish species (*Sciaenidae*) that can vibrate their swim bladders to produce drumming or croaking sounds.

elkhorn coral A kind of coral colony that grows in the shape of an elk's antler.

excursion line (also *expedition line, safety line*) A plastic rope made of polypropylene and strung just off the ocean bottom for use by divers to find their way to the safety of an underwater habitat in emergencies. A network of these ropes connects the **Aquarius** habitat to dive locations around **Conch Reef**.

Florida Keys National Marine Sanctuary An area of protected ocean habitat, encompassing 2,800 square **nautical miles** and extending into Florida Bay, the Gulf of Mexico, and the Atlantic Ocean. The sanctuary contains the third-largest coral barrier reef in the world.

freeze-dried food Fresh or cooked foods that are flash-frozen, then dried. They are easy to store and regain much of their original flavor when water is added.

global climate change A rise in the average temperature of Earth's surface caused by increasing amounts of water vapor, carbon dioxide, methane, and ozone, the so-called greenhouse gases. One of the destructive effects of global climate change is coral bleaching.

Hydrolab An underwater habitat and laboratory, the predecessor to **Aquarius**. Approximately 180 Hydrolab missions were conducted from the early 1970s to the mid-1980s.

kilometer Unit of linear measurement equal to about 0.62 **statute miles** or 0.54 **nautical miles**.

leaf coral A kind of coral colony or formation that is roughly in the shape of a leaf.

listening stations (also *acoustic receivers*) Listening stations that pick up sounds from pingers that have been attached to the animals that scientists want to track in the ocean.

Man-in-the-Sea Program A project begun in 1962 to establish manned undersea exploration. Inventor Edwin Link designed several submersible decompression chambers, the Submersible Portable Inflatable Dwelling (SPID), and the submersible Sea Link as part of the program.

Mission Control A 24-hour watch desk located on shore at Key Largo, Florida, for monitoring activity in and around the **Aquarius** habitat.

moon pool A section in the hull of research vessels that can be removed to give scientists direct access to the ocean, without flooding. In **Aquarius** the moon pool is essentially a hole in the floor through which divers enter and exit the habitat. Air pressure inside the **wet porch** keeps the ocean from flooding the living space.

national marine sanctuary One of thirteen areas of protected ocean habitat. The U.S. national marine sanctuaries range in size from less than one square nautical mile to more than 5,300 square nautical miles. Each sanctuary is a unique place needing special protections.

nautical mile Unit of measure equal to about 1.15 **statute miles** or about 1.85 **kilometers**.

NOAA (National Oceanic and Atmospheric Administration) A federal agency that, as part of the Department of Commerce, oversees policies for the oceans and the atmosphere.

off-gassing The slow release of nitrogen gas that builds up in the bloodstream during saturation diving. If released too quickly, the nitrogen can cause the **bends**.

Phoenix Island Protected Area The world's largest marine protected area, located near the equator in the Pacific Ocean between Fiji and Hawaii. This ocean wilderness area is about the size of the state of California and is part of the small Pacific Island nation of Kiribati.

pillar coral Tropical Atlantic coral that forms pillarlike spires as tall as 10 feet.

pinger (also *acoustic tag*) A tracking device that is attached to or surgically implanted in an animal and produces a signal that gives information about the animal's depth and location.

pistol shrimp (*Synalpheus* species; also called *large-claw snapping shrimp*) A coral reef shrimp that has one enlarged claw that makes a popping sound to catch food and scare off intruders.

saturation diving A diving technique in which a diver's body is permitted to absorb as much nitrogen and other inert gases as it can hold at a particular depth. This strategy allows nearly unlimited time to work underwater without further increasing decompression time.

scuba Acronym for self-contained underwater breathing apparatus. A device that allows divers to breathe and remain submerged in the water.

sea anemone Many-tentacled water animal related to corals and jellyfish. It uses its tentacles to catch and sting food.

Sealab Any of three underwater habitats built in the 1960s.

staghorn coral A kind of coral whose colonies have the shape of a deer's antlers, more slender and fingerlike than **elkhorn coral**.

Starfish House The main structure in an underwater explorers' village that was built in 1963 as part of underwater explorer Jacques Cousteau's **Conshelf** II program. Starfish House had the shape of a fat starfish wrapped in a steel skin. The program included a habitat called Deep Cabin, an underwater hangar for a hydrojet diving saucer (a two-man submersible), and a tool shed.

statute mile (also *land mile*) Unit of measure equal to 5,280 feet or about 0.87 **nautical miles** or about 1.6 **kilometers**.

swim bladder (also *gas bladder* or *air bladder*) A gas-filled organ inside a fish's body that helps the fish control its buoyancy.

underwater habitat A structure submerged in the ocean or freshwater lakes and ponds where people can work, sleep, eat, and rest for weeks at a time.

wet porch A space measuring 8 feet long, 12 feet wide, and 7 feet high inside the **Aquarius** habitat, just inside the **moon pool** entrance. In this space, **aquanauts** can go in and out of Aquarius, but air pressure keeps water from flowing up through the moon pool and flooding the undersea habitat.

Index (Pages in *italics* refer to captions.)

Image Credits

Photographs: The photographs on the front cover, back cover, and throughout this book were taken by Brian Skerry, with the following exceptions: pages 5 (top and bottom), 6 (bottom): Chris Newbert/Courtesy New England Aquarium; pages 12 (top), 15: Ashley Knight; pages 16, 17, 33: Kenneth Mallory; page 21: Courtesy of OAR/National Undersea Research Program (NUR), Dill Geomarine Assocs., NOAA Photo Library; page 30: Greg Stone; page 41: Paul Erickson.

Non-photographic images: page 4: John Nez; page 25: Terry Smith, after reference courtesy of the University of North Carolina, Wilmington; page 27: Jim Postier.